AMAZON
RAINFOREST

Galadriel Watson

www.av2books.com

AV² provides enriched content that supplements and complements this book. Weigl's AV² books strive to create inspired learning and engage young minds in a total learning experience.

Your AV² Media Enhanced books come alive with...

 Audio
Listen to sections of the book read aloud.

 Key Words
Study vocabulary, and complete a matching word activity.

 Video
Watch informative video clips.

 Quizzes
Test your knowledge.

 Embedded Weblinks
Gain additional information for research.

 Slideshow
View images and captions, and prepare a presentation.

 Try This!
Complete activities and hands-on experiments.

... and much, much more!

Go to www.av2books.com, and enter this book's unique code.

BOOK CODE

AVV76484

AV² by Weigl brings you media enhanced books that support active learning.

Published by AV² by Weigl
350 5th Avenue, 59th Floor
New York, NY 10118
Website: www.av2books.com   www.weigl.com

Library of Congress Control Number: 2019938452

ISBN 978-1-7911-0850-2 (hardcover)
ISBN 978-1-7911-0851-9 (softcover)
ISBN 978-1-7911-0852-6 (multi-user eBook)
ISBN 978-1-7911-0853-3 (single-user eBook)

Printed in Guangzhou, China
1 2 3 4 5 6 7 8 9 23 22 21 20 19

052019
311018

Project Coordinator Heather Kissock
Design Ana Maria Vidal and Tammy West

Every reasonable effort has been made to trace ownership and to obtain permission to reprint copyright material. The publishers would be pleased to have any errors or omissions brought to their attention so that they may be corrected in subsequent printings.

Photo Credits
Weigl acknowledges Getty Images, Alamy, iStock, Shutterstock, and Dreamstime as primary photo suppliers for this title.

AMAZON RAINFOREST

Contents

A Wealth of Life

With an area of more than 2 million square miles (5.2 million square kilometers), the Amazon rainforest in South America is the largest rainforest in the world. It is so large that it covers an area equal to about half of the United States. The Amazon rainforest is larger than the next two largest rainforests combined.

A wealth of plants and animals live in this vast region. In fact, more **species** of plants and animals live in the Amazon rainforest than in any other place on Earth. Fruits, nuts, coffee, and other foods are farmed in the Amazon. Certain plants are used to make important medicines. Thousands of types of monkeys, birds, insects, and other animals thrive in the rainforest's hot, wet climate.

Thousands of different types of orchids grow in the Amazon rainforest.

Poison dart frogs are brightly colored. These colors tell other animals not to eat the frogs.

Amazon Rainforest Facts

- Temperatures in the Amazon rainforest average about 80° Fahrenheit (27° Celsius), with up to 90 percent humidity. To humans, this feels like a steam bath.

- The Amazon region receives about 10 feet (3 meters) of rainfall per year. By comparison, the average U.S. city receives less than 3 feet (0.9 m) per year.

- The Amazon rainforest covers about one-third of the continent of South America.

- The rainforest surrounds the Amazon River, which is the second-longest river in the world. The Nile in Africa is the longest river in the world.

- The Amazon River carries 15 percent of the global river flow.

- The equator runs across the northern portion of the Amazon rainforest. Almost all of the world's tropical rainforests are located on or near the equator.

Mapping the Amazon Rainforest

Caribbean Sea

Amazon Rainforest

Atlantic Ocean

Pacific Ocean

SOUTH AMERICA

N
W
E
S

LEGEND
Water
Land
Amazon Rainforest
---- International Border

500 Miles

MAP SCALE 0

500 Km

Where in the World?

The Amazon rainforest is home to the 4,000-mile (6,437-km) Amazon River. It runs from the Andes Mountains to the Atlantic Ocean on the east coast of South America. Along the way, more than 1,000 **tributaries** feed into the Amazon. When the warm season arrives in the Andes, mountain snowmelt runs down to the Amazon. The already huge river swells and floods.

The Amazon rainforest surrounds the river. Much of the region is wild jungle, and few cities exist there. Part of the rainforest sits in the Tumucumaque Mountains National Park in Brazil. This protected area is the largest tropical forest national park in the world.

Turtles and butterflies are just a few of the animals that live mainly in or near the Amazon River.

The Amazon River can be up to 300 feet (100 m) deep in some areas.

Puzzler

Most of the Amazon rainforest lies in the country of Brazil, but it also extends into eight other countries. **Using an atlas or online source, review the map below and name each numbered country. The countries are listed in the box on the side.**

Atlantic Ocean

SOUTH AMERICA

Pacific Ocean

Atlantic Ocean

COUNTRIES
Bolivia
Brazil
Colombia
Ecuador
French Guiana
Guyana
Peru
Suriname
Venezuela

LEGEND
☐ Water
---- International Border

MAP SCALE 0 |———————| 400 Miles
|———————| 400 Km

N W E S

ANSWERS: 1. Peru **2.** Ecuador **3.** Colombia **4.** Venezuela **5.** Guyana **6.** Suriname **7.** French Guiana **8.** Brazil **9.** Bolivia

A Trip Back in Time

Millions of years ago, before humans lived on Earth, the Amazon River flowed west into the Pacific Ocean. Later, the region's tectonic plates, the rigid pieces of land that make up Earth's outer shell, began to shift. The tectonic shift pushed up huge masses of rock to form the Andes Mountains. With the mountains in its path, the Amazon River gradually found a new route. Eventually, the river moved east and reached the Atlantic Ocean. This change occurred about 8 million years ago.

In some parts of the world, such as North America, **ice age** glaciers covered the land and killed most living things. The Amazon, however, has never been covered by glaciers. This has allowed Amazon species to develop uninterrupted for millions of years.

The ceiba, or kapok, tree can grow to be 200 feet (61 m) tall and have a 10-foot (3-m) diameter.

The Andes Mountains stretch 5,500 miles (8,900 km) along the west coast of South America.

Rainforest Layers

The rainforest is divided into several layers, each with very different living conditions.

Emergents

Gigantic treetops rise above the rest of the forest's trees. Mostly birds and insects live here. This layer receives more sunlight than other layers.

Canopy

The treetops reach up to 165 feet (50 m). This area traps the most water and sunlight. These treetops produce the most food for the forest's creatures.

Understory

Here live shorter, younger trees that reach to about 60 feet (18 m). Only about 2 percent of sunlight reaches the understory.

Floor

The floor is dark. Only 0–2 percent of sunlight and very little water reach the floor. Few plants can grow in this darkness. The ground is covered with a layer of decomposing leaves and other matter called **humus**. Many fungi and insects live on the floor layer.

Plentiful Plants

Only a small amount of light and water reach the floor of the rainforest, so the soil is too poor to allow many plants to grow in the ground. In other environments, plants draw **nutrients** from the soil, but rainforest plants keep most nutrients in their leaves and tissues. They also receive nutrients from the floor's layer of humus.

Despite the poor soil, the Amazon rainforest holds countless types of plants. There are more than 2,500 species of trees. Many other plants make their homes in these trees. Lianas, which are a type of thick, woody vine, connect to young trees in the understory. They grow upward and attach themselves to taller branches. Some lianas grow as high as the canopy.

Some lianas are so thick that they could be mistaken for tree branches.

Trees in the Amazon do not have deep roots, because of the poor soil. Instead, they have shallow roots called buttress roots that grow widely across the ground.

The Rainy Season

The rainforest has two seasons, a rainy season and a dry season. The rainy season in the Amazon lasts about four months. There is still plenty of sunshine, but the clouds take every opportunity to release huge amounts of water. Also, during the rainy season, water from snow melting in the Andes runs down the mountains and flows into rivers and streams. Together, the rain and melted snow make for massive flooding in the rainforest. Vast areas of the forest floor are covered in water. Animals either climb trees or scramble to seek higher ground.

The dry season takes place during the Southern Hemisphere's winter months. The Amazon is still quite wet during this time, but the rain is far less frequent. This is when the floodwaters recede, allowing animals to return to the flooded land.

The southern part of the Amazon rainforest is typically the driest, but still receives plenty of rain.

Amazon Animals

Some incredible creatures live in the Amazon rainforest. Animals must be on guard against the anaconda, a huge water snake that kills its prey by wrapping its body around the other animal and squeezing it to death. One of the largest spiders in the world, the 10-inch (25-cm) bird-eating spider, lives in the Amazon, too. There are also many mammals, such as sloths, monkeys, and the vampire bat.

Scientists may never know exactly how many animals live in the Amazon. They estimate that there are about 1,300 bird species, 3,000 fish species, and 400 mammal species. Rainforest scientists often identify animal species that have never been known to humans. In the last 20 years, more than 2,000 new plant and animal species have been discovered in the Amazon region, and that number does not include insects. More than 20 of these new species are mammals. They include a pink river dolphin and the fire-tailed titi monkey.

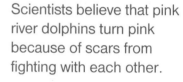

Scientists believe that pink river dolphins turn pink because of scars from fighting with each other.

The green anaconda is the largest snake in the world by weight. It can weigh up to 550 pounds (250 kilograms).

Endangered Species

Some scientists estimate that about 200 plant and animal species become extinct every day. This means if the last member of the species dies, the species will never return to life again. Extinction is caused by changes in the ecosystem. Some causes are natural. Others are caused by humans.

The Amazon's jaguar population is currently in danger. Local ranchers kill jaguars if they suspect the cats have been attacking their herds. Hunters also kill jaguars for their fur.

A threatened plant species is the mahogany tree. People around the world love furniture made of the dark reddish-brown mahogany wood. The trees are cut down so frequently that mahogany might soon become extinct in the Amazon.

Jaguars are difficult to track in the wild, but it is estimated that about 10,000 live in the Amazon.

Researching the Forest

The Amazon rainforest canopy holds many mysteries. Since the canopy is so hard to reach, scientists have studied it less than the ocean floor. However, they believe that 60 to 90 percent of the rainforest's animal and plant life live in the canopy.

In the 1800s, European explorers hired **indigenous** peoples to climb the trees and bring down samples of plant life. Presently, scientists can measure trees using **lasers**. They also use **satellite** pictures to study large areas of the forest. In recent years, scientists have built platforms high in the trees so they can get a closeup look at canopy life. One scientist even developed a canopy "raft," a large platform that floats in the air. It is held up by helium-filled tubes.

Satellite images help scientists track changes to the forest.

Biography

Henry Walter Bates (1825–1892)

Henry Walter Bates spent more than a decade studying nature in the Amazon rainforest. Bates was a naturalist, a scientist who studies nature. He was the first person to identify about 8,000 rainforest insects. Bates described his findings in his book, *The Naturalist on the River Amazons*, which was published in 1863.

Bates was well known for his studies on insect mimicry. Mimicry is when a species of animal looks like another species so that **predators** cannot easily see the animal. For example, the viceroy butterfly, which is eaten by birds, looks like the monarch butterfly, which birds hate to eat. Since the viceroy looks like the monarch, birds often leave the viceroy alone. This animal trait is called "Batesian mimicry," named after Bates.

Henry Walter Bates first arrived in Brazil in 1848. He collected more than 14,000 species during his time in the Amazon.

Facts of Life

- Born: February 8, 1825
- Hometown: Leicester, England
- Occupation: Naturalist
- Died: February 16, 1892

The Big Picture

The Amazon rainforest is one of several rainforests in the world. The largest rainforests are in Central and South America, Asia, and Africa. Although these forests cover only about 7 percent of Earth's land, they are home to more than 50 percent of its plant and animal species.

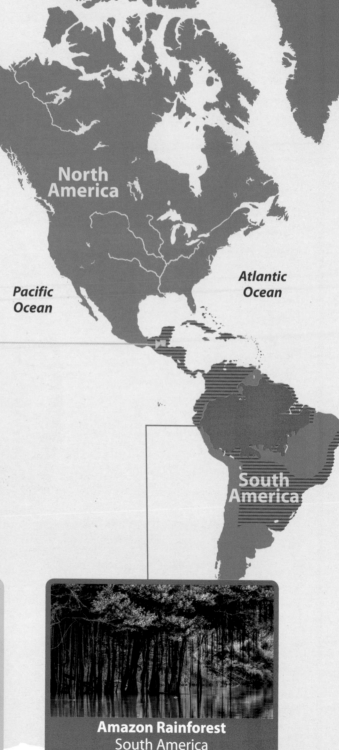

North America

Pacific Ocean

Atlantic Ocean

South America

LEGEND

- Water
- Land
- Antarctica
- Rainforest

N
W   E
S

MAP SCALE   0 |————————| 2,000 Miles
                        2,000 Km

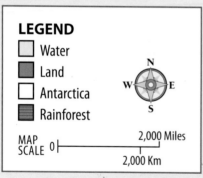

Maya Biosphere Reserve
Guatemala, Central America

Amazon Rainforest
South America

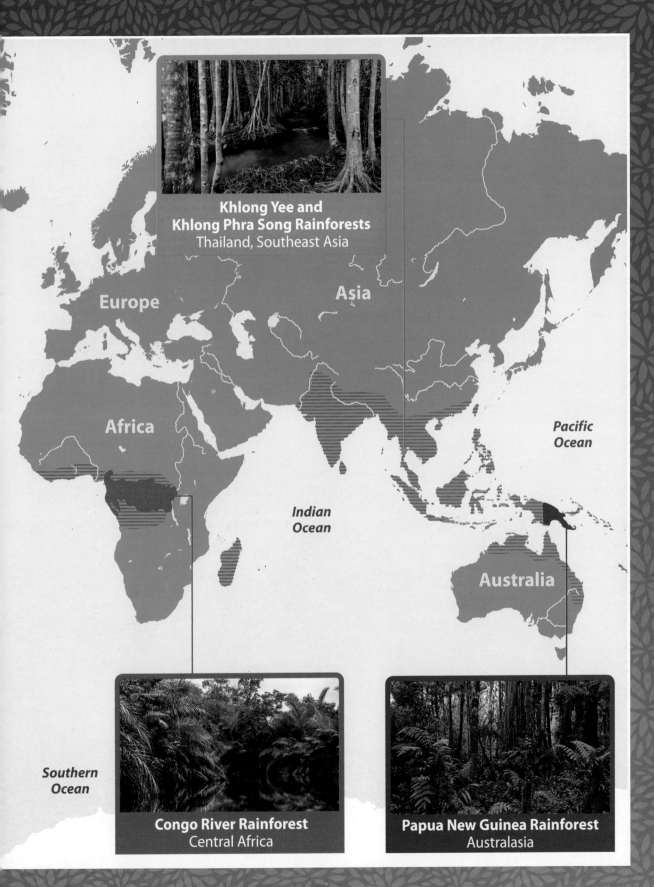

**Khlong Yee and
Khlong Phra Song Rainforests**
Thailand, Southeast Asia

Europe

Asia

Africa

*Pacific
Ocean*

*Indian
Ocean*

Australia

*Southern
Ocean*

Congo River Rainforest
Central Africa

Papua New Guinea Rainforest
Australasia

People of the Amazon

The first people to live in the Amazon arrived thousands of years ago. When Spanish conquerors called conquistadors arrived in the 1500s, they destroyed many of these ancient civilizations. Francisco de Orellana was the first European to explore the Amazon.

Today, about 30 million people live in the Amazon region. About half of these people live in cities. The city of Manaus, Brazil, has a population of about 2 million. The city of Belém has a population of about 1.4 million, and more than 2 million live in the Belém metropolitan region. Many other people of the Amazon region are farmers or gold prospectors. Approximately 2.7 million are indigenous peoples. They belong to more than 350 ethnic groups, such as the Yanomami, the Xikrin, and the Juruna.

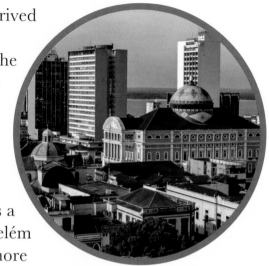

Manaus is a busy city, where many tourists begin their journey into the Amazon region.

The Yanomami live in small villages where they grow their own crops and also hunt.

Puzzler

Since the Amazon rainforest is crisscrossed with waterways, and because so much of it floods during the rainy season, the best way to travel is by boat. Native peoples still make their own, just as they have for centuries. **From what material are the Amazon canoes called *pirogues* made?**

ANSWER: These boats are made from hollowed tree trunks.

Timeline

90 million years ago
The Andes Mountains begin to form.

1500s
European explorers first arrive in the Amazon basin.

10,000–15,000 years ago
The Amazon's earliest inhabitants arrive.

| 90 million years ago | 8 million years ago | 10,000–15,000 years ago | 1500 | 1600 | 1700 |

8 million years ago
The Amazon River breaks through to the Atlantic Ocean.

1740s
Europeans in the Amazon discover **latex**, which becomes a key substance in producing rubber and plastic products.

2005
The Amazon experiences a severe drought. Thousands of square miles (sq. km) burn.

2010
A new species of long-tailed monkey is discovered in Mato Grosso, Brazil.

| 1875 | 1900 | 1925 | 1950 | 1975 | 2000 | 2025 |

1863
Henry Walter Bates publishes his book *The Naturalist on the River Amazons*.

2018
The World Wildlife Foundation estimates that more than 25 percent of the Amazon **biome** will be without trees by 2030.

2002
The Brazilian government announces the creation of Tumucumaque Mountains National Park.

Key Issue

The Disappearing Forest

The Amazon rainforest is disappearing at an alarming rate. From August 2017 to July 2018, about 3,050 square miles (7,900 sq. km) of rainforest were cut or burned just in Brazil. This area is larger than the size of the state of Delaware. **Deforestation** is a difficult issue because there are both good and bad reasons to clear trees. For instance, the wood from these trees makes products such as furniture and flooring. This brings money into the area economies. On the other hand, deforestation destroys some animals' habitats.

The rate of deforestation in the Brazilian part of the Amazon in 2018 was the worst it had been in the last decade.

Governments and businesses try to replace some of the deforested areas. However, the ecosystems that grow in these newer forests contain fewer plant and animal species. Once an ancient rainforest area is cleared, it is likely gone forever.

A plan to plant 73 million trees in Brazil began in 2017 and is expected to take six years.

Should trees be cut down in the Amazon rainforest?

Yes	No
The world's population is increasing and needs wood for fuel and timber.	Countless plant and animal species are wiped out by deforestation.
Selling rainforest trees brings much-needed income into the region.	Indigenous peoples lose their homes and eventually forget important knowledge about the land, its species, and its history.
Land needs to be cleared to build new settlements so people can move out of overcrowded cities.	The loss of trees causes local air temperatures to rise, reduces the amount of rain in the area, and increases the level of **carbon dioxide** in the atmosphere. These factors all contribute to the **greenhouse effect**.

Deforestation in other Amazonian countries, such as Bolivia and Peru, is also increasing.

Natural Attractions

Tourists who visit the Amazon rainforest are vital to its survival for many reasons. Perhaps most importantly, tourism brings money to people who have little. Visitors spend money on hotels, food, and local products. Also, tourism encourages the local inhabitants to properly care for the wilderness so it will continue to attract visitors. Some hotels have built walkways and platforms to allow tourists to observe the canopy ecosystem just as scientists are able to do.

Ziplining is another way tourists can travel through the canopy.

The vast rainforest offers visitors many different opportunities for exploration. Some people travel to the Meeting of the Waters, a place where the dark and light waters of two rivers run side-by-side without mixing. Others visit Lake Janauari Ecological Park to see giant water lilies, measuring up to 7 feet (2.1 m) across.

River cruises take tourists out on the water to see the dark water of the Rio Negra and the sand-colored water of the Amazon River meet.

Be Prepared

A visit to the Amazon rainforest can be a rough and rugged trip, but with proper preparation, it can be safe, fascinating, and the experience of a lifetime.

It is important to dress for very hot temperatures and high humidity. Loose-fitting cotton clothing is best.

If traveling on foot through the forest floor, some tour companies recommend bringing "mud shoes," an old pair of inexpensive sneakers.

Since most of the animals reside high in the canopy, a pair of binoculars is the best way to see them.

Many areas of the forest floor receive little sunlight even during daytime, so a flashlight will help in the dark.

A rainforest visit will not be spent entirely in the shade. Be prepared for sunny spots by bringing sunscreen, a hat, and sunglasses.

Be sure to bring insect repellent.

Heavy rains can occur at any time, so a good raincoat or poncho is needed.

Visitors should always have a camera ready. Tourists cannot take plants or animals home from the rainforest, but they can take as many pictures as they want.

Local Knowledge

Over the thousands of years that indigenous peoples have lived in the Amazon, they have come to know many of the plants and their uses. Some of this knowledge has spread to other parts of the world. This makes many Amazon plants desirable.

For example, Brazil nuts, pineapples, and cocoa are popular foods from the Amazon region. Rubber taken from the Amazon's rubber trees is used in many places around the world, as well. Guaraná is a drink made from an Amazonian seed that has up to five times more **caffeine** than coffee. Doctors treat the disease malaria with a medicine called quinine, which comes from the bark of the Amazon's cinchona tree. Drug companies around the world use many other key ingredients from Amazon plants to make important, life-saving medicines.

People who work as rubber tree tappers carve lines into the bark of rubber trees that lead down to a bucket, to collect the substance needed to make rubber.

Guaraná Antarctica is a popular soft drink originally from Brazil that is made with guaraná.

Amazon Mythology

Manioc is another name for cassava, a starchy root used to make flour. According to local mythology, manioc has magical beginnings. The legend says that long ago, the daughter of a Native chieftain gave birth to a beautiful boy, whom she named Mani. Mani was loved very much, but he died at three years of age. Mani's mother buried him near her house and wept over his grave. Eventually, a plant began to grow from the grave. The plant was named manioc, after the little boy Mani.

Manioc is poisonous if eaten raw and can make people sick if not cooked or prepared properly.

What Have You Learned?

True or False?

Decide whether the following statements are true or false. If the statement is false, make it true.

1. Henry Walter Bates was a conquistador.

2. According to legend, manioc is named after a boy named Mani.

3. People know much more about the rainforest canopy than the ocean floor.

4. The Amazon's jaguar population is increasing.

5. Humus is made partly of decomposing leaves.

6. Income from tourism encourages local people to take care of the Amazon wilderness.

ANSWERS: 1. False. He was a naturalist. **2.** True **3.** False. They know less about the canopy. **4.** False. The jaguar population is decreasing. **5.** True **6.** True

Short Answer

Answer the following questions using information from the book.

1. To what ocean does the Amazon River flow?

2. What did not cover the Amazon during an ice age?

3. What are the names of the rainforest's layers?

4. What are lianas?

5. What drink has more caffeine than coffee?

ANSWERS: 1. The Atlantic Ocean **2.** Glaciers **3.** Emergents, Canopy, Understory, Floor **4.** Thick, woody vines **5.** Guaraná

Multiple Choice

Choose the best answer for the following questions.

1. The Amazon rainforest is mostly in:

    a. Mexico
    b. Brazil
    c. Ecuador
    d. Argentina

2. Pirogues are a type of:

    a. food
    b. flower
    c. fish
    d. boat

3. What group of indigenous peoples lives in the Amazon?

    a. The Yanomami
    b. The San
    c. The Aztecs
    d. The Mohawks

4. What do doctors use as a treatment for malaria?

    a. Brazil nut
    b. Guaraná
    c. Curare
    d. Quinine

ANSWERS: 1. b 2. d 3. a 4. d

Activity

Rubber from the Rainforest

Many indigenous families make their living tapping rubber trees in the Amazon rainforest. Rubber comes from a milky white substance inside the trees. Tapping them does not kill the tree, and a rubber tree can be tapped for about 20 years. Try this experiment to make your own rubber-like material.

Materials

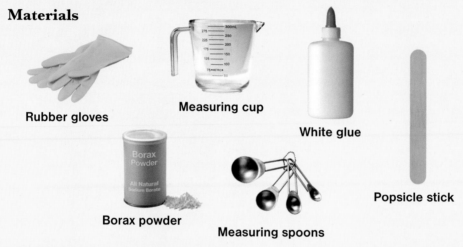

Rubber gloves

Measuring cup

White glue

Popsicle stick

Borax powder

Measuring spoons

Instructions

1. Put on rubber or latex gloves to protect your hands.

2. Mix 1 cup (237 ml) of water with 1 tablespoon (15 ml) of borax.

3. In a separate plastic container, thoroughly mix 1-2/3 tablespoons (25 ml) of white glue with 1-1/3 tablespoons (20 ml) of water.

4. Add 1 teaspoon (5 ml) of the borax solution into the glue-and-water mixture. Stir with the Popsicle stick. When a solid substance has adhered to the stick, peel it off and knead it onto a paper towel until it loses its stickiness.

Results

A rubbery material will be formed. It will have the consistency of putty. Try stretching it. Form it into a ball, and bounce it. Think about the many daily uses for rubber, at home, at school, and in industries around the world.

Key Words

biome: a large naturally occurring habitat, such as a forest

caffeine: a substance in plants such as coffee and tea that, when consumed, can make people feel alert

carbon dioxide: a gas that is found normally in the atmosphere and is absorbed by plants

deforestation: the act of removing trees from an area

greenhouse effect: the dangerous warming of Earth

humus: a brownish, mushy substance made up of dead, decomposing parts of plants and animal waste on a forest floor

ice age: a period of time when a large area of Earth is covered by glaciers

indigenous: native to a certain place; having been born in a place

lasers: devices that emit a beam of radiation

latex: a liquid produced by certain types of plants that is made into rubber

nutrients: any substance that provides nourishment when consumed

predators: animals that hunt and kill other animals for food

satellite: a spacecraft that travels around Earth and transmits communication signals

species: specific groups of plants or animals that share characteristics

tributaries: bodies of water that feed into larger bodies of water, such as rivers

Index

Log on to www.av2books.com

AV² by Weigl brings you media enhanced books that support active learning. Go to www.av2books.com, and enter the special code found on page 2 of this book. You will gain access to enriched and enhanced content that supplements and complements this book. Content includes video, audio, weblinks, quizzes, a slideshow, and activities.

AV² Online Navigation

Audio
Listen to sections of the book read aloud.

Book Pages
AV² pages directly correspond to pages in the book.

Video
Watch informative video clips.

Embedded Weblinks
Gain additional information for research.

Key Words
Study vocabulary, and complete a matching word activity.

Try This!
Complete activities and hands-on experiments.

Quizzes
Test your knowledge.

Slideshow
View images and captions, and prepare a presentation.

AV² was built to bridge the gap between print and digital. We encourage you to tell us what you like and what you want to see in the future.

Sign up to be an AV² Ambassador at www.av2books.com/ambassador.

Due to the dynamic nature of the internet, some of the URLs and activities provided as part of AV² by Weigl may have changed or ceased to exist. AV² by Weigl accepts no responsibility for any such changes. All media enhanced books are regularly monitored to update addresses and sites in a timely manner. Contact AV² by Weigl at 1-866-649-3445 or av2books@weigl.com with any questions, comments, or feedback.